Great Wall of China

by Grace Hansen

Abdo
WORLD WONDERS
Kids

abdopublishing.com

Published by Abdo Kids, a division of ABDO, P.O. Box 398166, Minneapolis, Minnesota 55439.

Printed in the United States of America, North Mankato, Minnesota.

102017

012018

THIS BOOK CONTAINS RECYCLED MATERIALS

Photo Credits: Granger Collection, iStock, Shutterstock

Production Contributors: Teddy Borth, Jennie Forsberg, Grace Hansen

Design Contributors: Dorothy Toth, Laura Mitchell

Publisher's Cataloging in Publication Data

Names: Hansen, Grace, author.

Title: Great Wall of China / by Grace Hansen.

Description: Minneapolis, Minnesota : Abdo Kids, 2018. | Series: World wonders |
Includes glossary, index and online resource (page 24).

Identifiers: LCCN 2017943218 | ISBN 9781532104411 (lib.bdg.) | ISBN 9781532105531 (ebook) |
ISBN 9781532106095 (Read-to-me ebook)

Subjects: LCSH: Great Wall of China (China)--Juvenile literature. | China--Great Wall of China--Juvenile literature. |Great Wall of China (China)--History--Juvenile literature.

Classification: DDC 951--dc23

LC record available at https://lccn.loc.gov/2017943218

Table of Contents

The Great Wall of China

The Great Wall is in China. It runs throughout northern China.

China

Early parts of the wall were built more than 2,000 years ago. Qin Shi Huang was the first **Emperor** of China. He wanted a large wall to protect the country.

Other **dynasties** continued to build after Qin. Most of the wall was made during the Ming dynasty.

Thousands of people worked on the wall. Most of them were **peasants** and criminals. It was very hard work. Many died.

The wall is made up of many materials. Wood, soil, pebbles, and twigs make up walls in the **plains**. In the desert, the wall is made from **adobe** and dirt. Walls in mountains are made from rock, clay, and more.

The Great Wall is made up of many shorter walls. In total, it measures more than 13,000 miles (21,000 km)!

Thousands of watchtowers line the Great Wall. From there, smoke and fire signals warned of attacks.

The Qing **dynasty** had no use for the wall. And after China became a **Republic**, leaders ignored it. They thought it was a sign of cruelty.

Restoration

In 1976, Deng Xiaoping was elected. He saw the wall as a **symbol** of China's strength. Repairs to the wall began, mostly near Beijing. Today, it is a popular place to visit!

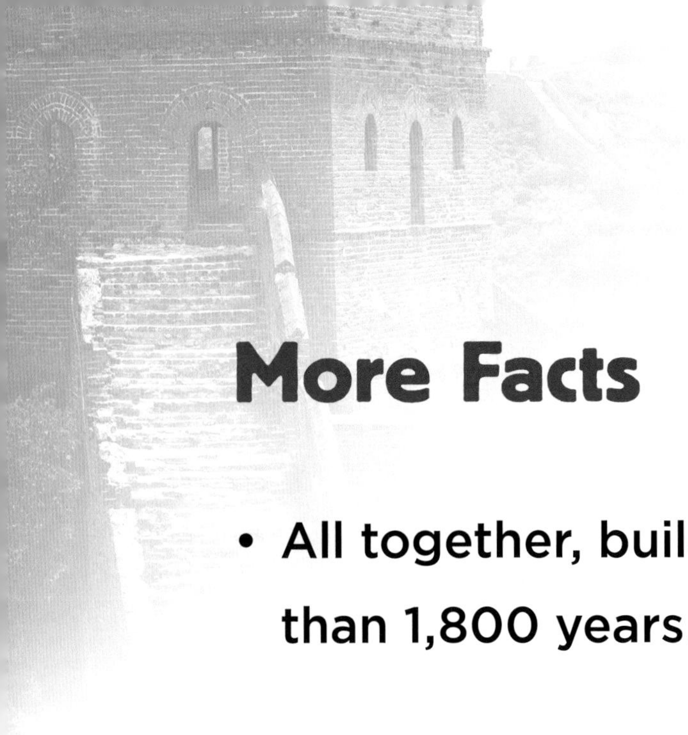

More Facts

- All together, building the Great Wall took more than 1,800 years.
- The average height of the wall is around 22 feet (6.7 m). The tallest parts of the wall are 46 feet (14 m) high.
- Nearly 1/3 of the Great Wall has disappeared over the years.

Glossary

adobe – sun-dried brick made from clay and straw.

dynasty – a series of rulers from the same family or group.

emperor – the male ruler of an empire.

peasant – a member of the class of farm workers in Asia.

plains – a large, flat area of land without trees.

Republic – a nation in which those who make the laws and run the government are elected by the people.

symbol – an object that represents something else.

Index